To
Rebe

Don't Let the
the
Idiots Win!

Don't Let the Idiots Win!

Ten Easy Steps to Building Relationships and Finishing Strong in Life

Jeff Denton

Illustrated by Richard Smith

Finishing Strong Productions
PONCA CITY, OKLAHOMA

First printing 2002

ISBN 0-9718063-0-6
LCCN 2002090772

ATTENTION CORPORATIONS, UNIVERSITIES, COLLEGES, AND PROFESSIONAL ORGANIZATIONS: Quantity discounts are available on bulk purchases of this book for educational, gift purposes, or as premiums for increasing magazine subscriptions or renewals. Special books or book excerpts can also be created to fit specific needs. For information, please contact Finishing Strong Productions, P.O. Box 773, Ponca City, OK 74602.; ph. 580-765-3345.

DEDICATION

Thank you to Sissy and Sherrie, for their wealth of inspiration and encouragement in making this book possible, and for living each and every experience.

Thanks to my wife Camille, for staying married to "a piece of work" and dreaming the dream with me.

Thanks to my son Jordan and my daughter Madison, for sharing their dad with many others.

Finally, special thanks to my mom and dad, for living the perfect example—not just the words but living the life. Dad would have been proud!

TABLE OF CONTENTS

INTRODUCTION

It was a rainy summer day in central Colorado. I decided to get a bite to eat at a quaint restaurant, while visiting the old town casino area of Central City.

It had been the year of all years. One problem after another, munching on my hindquarters, like a football team at an all-you-can-eat buffet. I was amazed I had the ability to bend my rear into the chair—or that I even had a rear to bend at all!

We all have experienced those extended periods when "people problems" just physically wear us out. You know, the metaphoric ripping of body tissue that seems to last longer than the time it takes the airplane to get from the landing strip to the gate.

I sat in the hardwood chair, looked across the table at my coworkers and friends, Liz and Cheryl. It was like the first part of the conversation occurred in my head and the only vocal part appeared to come just out of the blue. The only thing they heard was an odd statement disguised as a question: "Why do the idiots always win?"

The spewing of iced tea and initial laughter turned quickly to surrendering sighs, indicating a grave realization we had just completed a year that set the record for what we would later call "idiot attacks." Each of us had a defeated look on our face, finally accepting we apparently had no control over the unannounced incoming sorties, displacing the scattering of buckshot inflicting massive internal damage.

As if I was portraying the role of a losing coach at halftime, I uttered a statement of disgust. "We let it happen to us! We sat there and allowed the idiots to take complete control of our situation. We just watched like we were spectators of the entire event.

"Why do the idiots always win? Why do we just watch it happen? Where is it written that we have to sit back and watch the mutilations and not think we have any rights?"

We all looked at each other and at the same time, as if we had rehearsed the response, we painfully stated, "It's because we let them." Plain and simple. *We let them.*

I felt like a television evangelist closing his message with a soft and sad yet confident response to his own question. "Why do the idiots always win? We let them! We let them reach inside our hearts and play idiot Kong."

From that point, I decided, no more! If I was to be the dad, husband, friend and employee God intended me to be, then I was going to have to either crawl in a hole or change the way I did things. Otherwise, the munching of my hind end would work its way to the rest of my body until there were just tired, old bones.

I knew I could come up with a solution because I was not blaming this on anyone but me. Society has a way of blaming everyone else for its problems, but the key to this entire thing was to change what I was doing, then to educate others on how we all can keep the idiots from winning.

I asked the waiter for a napkin, borrowed a pen from Liz and began a list that has evolved into what we now call *Anti-Idiotologies.*

Over the course of several years, items have been added, some modified and others deleted until there were ten statements demonstrating behavior characteristics and how we can keep the idiots from winning.

I decided to call the ten-step plan *Don't Let the Idiots Win!* Upon hearing this title many people gasp and say, "I can't believe you are calling certain people idiots. How arrogant, unkind, insensitive and downright rude. Have you no compassion?" I just gently state that idiots are not specific people but simply the way people act, react and deal with life. Ironically, it's the way I act, respond and deal with life.

Recognizing how we let the idiots win is the first step in learning how to not be an idiot target. If we see the scuds coming in, we can fire the anti-idiot missiles and shoot down these flying bombs before they do any damage.

Each person must realize that the entire responsibility of defeating the idiots lies solely on his or her shoulders. This is probably why many have trouble deflecting the idiot attacks. It is simply easier to ignore, give in or roll over when shots are being fired. However, history has proved that when there is no defense, damage is long-term and almost impossible to overcome.

Understanding and recognizing these ten "anti-idiotologies" can bring ongoing relief in the process of living life to its fullest, without constantly nursing wounds and cleaning up the mess from the attacks.

If you are tired of being an "idiot target," join me on this journey through the world of idiotologies.

DEFINITIONS

Idiots: These are not specific people, but specific actions by people. The reference to an "idiot" is really like giving a virus carrier a name. The references are directed toward the *behavior* of a person, not the individual.

Idiot behavior: A behavior invoked on you by someone else that causes you to respond in a way that you regret later, or in a manner that is conflicting with your foundational belief of faith and character.

Idiot shield: Preventative actions you take to deflect the attacks and minimize the damage.

Anti-Idiotologies: A set of life-skill assumptions that if understood and followed can result in a happier and healthier life in this world.

Pity huckster: One who seeks out, loves and makes a living off of pity from other people.

CHAPTER 1

Sticky Note Syndrome

We have all been there. You know, the rosy road of personal motivation. Books, videos, seminars, sermons and Oprah. Each of us has a desire to improve various aspects of our lives. Really, we all do! If you don't believe it, just watch late night television. The airwaves are cluttered with an incredible amount of self-help products, including exercise equipment, psychics, talk shows and books like this one.

Unfortunately, it usually ends shortly after we close the book, rewind the video, pull out of the parking lot of the seminar or church or when the "Jerry Springer Show" begins. It's not that we mean to disregard this feel-good stuff. It just doesn't stick very long.

It's called the "sticky note" syndrome. Good ideas stick for a moment, but any rustling of the papers, a slight shift of the wind and goodbye sticky note. It's a good thing our good intentions don't litter our floor-boards like our sticky notes do.

Or do they?

New Year's Day is probably the best example. We all set out to accomplish specific things in the next year and we target New Year's Day as the first day of the rest of our lives. After all, what a great target date! What better day to start a diet, a new attitude and challenging career goals?

Now let's break it down why this time is so good for our new plans.

We have been on a six-week food binge, entertained family and friends until we hate to hear the phone or doorbell ring and most of our thoughts of work are only vaguely present. We are ready for change in many undesirable parts of our lives. Let's face it; sticky note syndrome is just around the corner. Just waiting for us to tear a note off of the pad, write down a quick comment and stick it right in the middle of our forehead.

So why do these "self-help" things seem not to stick? Does this mean we are bad people? That we don't care? Are we lazy and unable to keep a commitment?

Well, in all honesty, it sure does!

Isn't it about time to get off the baby food and on to some real meat and taters? The truth is, we just don't want to look this big, ugly monster in the eye. We are afraid!

Don't you just hate the truth?

My dentist at the voodoo village had a sign on the wall across from the reclining torture chair. The meaning was very clear: "Be true to your teeth, and they won't be false to you." It sure made me want to stay in that chair and trade short-term pain for long-term gain.

Isn't it about time we quit trying to fool ourselves into thinking ignoring what goes on in our relationships has no effect on our mental health? (See Anti-Idiotology # 9.)

If I didn't know any better, I would think we are a society of "pity hucksters." That's right, pity hucksters. Now before you start doing your righteous ha-rumph, ha-rumph (borrowed from the movie *Blazing Saddles*), let me give you the definition of a pity huckster. The world is full of them. They come in all shapes, sizes and colors. In fact, I was one. I received my master's degree in the art of being one. It's not difficult. All you have to do is use your life experiences in a sad and pitiful way to get people to pay attention to you. Whether the attention is positive or negative, you get something out of the whole ordeal. We see this often in the classroom; negative attention is as good as positive attention. It can be a number of experiences—illnesses, relationships (that's where I really was good), jobs and physical attributes.

The first step in not letting the idiots win is understanding that we don't benefit at all from the pity of others. It has no emotional value.

I remember when you could deduct all of the interest from your consumer credit cards on your income tax. My brother, who is a top-notch accountant, read me the riot act when I was delighted by the fact that I had so much paid interest to deduct on my taxes. He looked me in the eye, like only a brother and accountant can, and said, "Being happy about how much interest you paid on a credit card is stupid." He was right. Paying for a consumer purchase three or four times the actual value is not a good thing at all.

Neither is living off of the pity of the way someone is treating you. It serves no purpose. It only keeps the wounds open and they rarely ever heal.

So stop it! Grab a tube of superglue and generously apply to your sticky notes and let's get going on how to keep the idiots from winning!

R. SMith

CHAPTER 2

Sock It to Me... Sock It to Me... Sock It to Me!

Anti-Idiotology #1:
Don't Let Yourself Be Upset
by Things Said by Those You
Don't R-E-S-P-E-C-T!

The sixties song by Aretha Franklin sums it up well: "R-E-S-P-E-C-T. Sock it to me. Sock it to me. Sock it to me."

Unfortunately the reverse seems to happen in relationships. When we let ourselves become upset by things said by those we don't respect, it's almost as if we open up our hearts and say, "Sock it to me, sock it to me, sock it to me."

I realize it is easier said than done to not let these non-factors launch their scuds into our emotions. That is why this Anti-Idiotology is number one. If you can lick this one, you are well on your way to not letting the idiots win.

13

Assessing

The best defense is to ask yourself, "Why do I value this person's opinions and what positive effect do they have on my life?"

If they spend a lot of time dumping their garbage in your emotional container, they probably are not adding any value to your life.

These people are all over. They usually are casual acquaintances who waltz in and out of your life, dropping bombs and moving on. Usually their mode of operation is to not stick around after the initial attack. Once you get the mess cleaned up, they fly back in, drop another bomb, then move on.

For some reason, we seem to find some value to these people. It's almost as if we become dependent on them setting us straight. Why don't we just paint a big red and white target on our chest and dare them to fire a shot.

Incoming

As I sat at a faculty lunch table, a teacher was having a conversation with another female coworker. The two had been at odds on various small issues for the past several months. Out of the blue, one of the women loudly said, "Do you know my mom is only four years older than you?"

My initial response of laughter was probably not the best, but it seemed like the only thing that would crack the uncomfortable frigid silence. After I realized everyone at the table except the combatants was male, I immediately stopped laughing. (Well, not really.) When two females go after each other verbally, and you're the only man laughing, well....

I waited a moment, then glanced in the direction of a friend. Without moving my lips, I whispered, "That was good." In the same tone, he whispered back to me, "I will have to give her a ten on that one."

I know that simple "buzz bomb" remark really did some damage. There was no advance warning to put up the defenses ahead of time. The anti-idiot guns would have not helped in this situation, but they would after the fact.

To this day, there is no respect between those two. I assume both have moved on, but it was very apparent at the moment the receiver was bothered by the remark. *Damage done!*

I have always been hypersensitive to what people say to me. As a child, I was always having a pity party over some remark. As a sixth-grader, I hung around with the coolest kid in the class. We were best friends. One night, we ventured out of his parents' house and headed down the alley to visit the most popular girls in the class. When we arrived at their house, they were standing on the front porch smoking cigarettes. The girls let my best friend take a drag of their Virginia Slims but did not even acknowledge my presence or ask me if I wanted to take a drag. I got tired of waiting for their offer, so I asked if I could have a "hit." One of the girls looked at me and said, "Your face is dirty and you are too ugly to smoke my cigarette." I was crushed. Not because I couldn't take a hit off of the cigarette, but because she really hurt my feelings.

From that point on, I let her little remark dictate to me how I perceived everyone felt about me. I let her air-to-ground missile (she was taller than me) do a lot of damage to my self-esteem for years to come. Ironically, I saw her at my 20th class reunion and was delighted to note that I had raised my standards much higher than hers.

We choose our responses to other people's comments and actions.

No one makes us react in any specific manner. We determine our reaction and actions based on our own mental conditioning. Allowing others to control our self-concept and value only validates their specific comments and position.

It all comes down to respect. Don't let yourself be upset by things said by those you don't R-E-S-P-E-C-T!

CHAPTER 3

Oh Baby, Let Me Be Your Chameleon Friend

Anti-Idiotology #2:
Don't Let Another Person's Mood Dictate How You Feel About Yourself!

According to the *Encarta Encyclopedia,* "chameleon" is a common name for certain lizards that are well known for their ability to change colors. The chameleon changes color when it is frightened and in response to light, temperature and other environmental shifts. The color change is caused by hormones that affect special pigment-bearing cells in the skin. Its color does not always change to match its surroundings, however, as is commonly believed.

As humans, we spend a lot of time adapting to our environment. We are constantly sorting out the data sent to us through conversation, body language and observation. Like the chameleon, we often change ourselves based on a change in the environment. If you don't believe this, just watch a person walk in a room when everyone is laughing and observe the smile break out on his face upon entering the room. We are good at assuming the ambiance of our environment. Have you ever been present in body at a meeting or workshop and caught yourself clapping with the rest of the group, even though you have no idea why you are clapping?

The Funeral Singer

I sing at a lot of funerals. It's not anything I put on my resume, but it seems to be an area in which I excel. Maybe it's not that I am good at singing, it's just that I am willing to volunteer for this hazardous duty. It's the one time when people crying while you are singing can be a good thing. However, singing at funerals can be difficult because of all the distractions and emotions during the service.

There are two ways to sing at a funeral. One is to hide in the back and look at a wall and sing. It's kind of like singing in the shower without the sound of water and good acoustics. The other is to stand right in the middle of a platform and stare at the audience and sing. It seems like the deceased person's family always requests me to sing all four verses of a very slow song. This is worse than water torture because of the amount of time spent in front of everyone during such a sad time.

The out-in-front method is more meaningful but much more difficult. It never serves the family well to have the vocalist break down during the song.

Busting out bawling can totally send the entire con-gregation into a sobbing mess. I know by experience this can happen.

So, the entire time I sing, I have to almost disen-gage myself from the situation. There are basic rules to accomplish this objective, but the biggest is to not make eye contact with the family or anyone who is crying in the crowd.

If I ever make eye contact—well, just kiss the song goodbye.

I don't mean to compare our daily jobs to the seriousness of a funeral service, but there are some major similarities in handling the two situations. Maybe we can take a lesson from the funeral singer.

Here is how it works: Oftentimes we walk right into these "idiot" ambushes. It happens on a regular basis. You know, you're just minding your own busi-ness and all of a sudden the enemy fire changes our scouting mission to an all-out war. Somehow, some-way we take on their mood, attitude and demeanor.

Almost every organization has its own "toxic cess-pool." It's the department, site or division everyone hates to venture through. These toxic sites usually have gatekeepers or greeters who snatch defeat out of the jaws of victory at a moment's notice. Before we know it, we assume their demeanor. We adapt their tone, attitude and disposition. It's as if they possess our body and take over our being. This hap-pens at the job, church or home.

My wife doesn't like to hear a commonly used Oklahoma saying that states, "If momma ain't happy, ain't no one happy." Realistically, this is a very true statement. Mom or Dad can set the emotional tempo of the household. We have the ability to fly in and make an attack, then fly right out before anybody can do a thing.

Dealing with not allowing someone else's mood to dictate how you feel about yourself is easy to talk about but difficult to actually accomplish.

If we can be like the funeral singer and not allow ourselves to be emotionally drawn into the situation, then we can be successful in not adopting someone else's gloom and doom. We need to assess the situation, prior, during and after the toxic poisoning. It's important we become aware of the possibility of being contaminated by a negative attitude. Recognizing that this could happen is the first step in not assuming their negative behavior.

A final note: If you forget the words of the song while singing at a funeral, just hum! Doo be doo be da da!

CHAPTER 4

Wiseguy

Anti-Idiotology #3:
Wisdom Is the Art of
Knowing What to Overlook!
...Don't Overlook Everything!

Every day we process an endless amount of data sent to our emotional and analytical hubs. Our brains are incredible. We make snap decisions on how we react to all kinds of stimuli. It's as if we have these little buckets we dump the data in for safekeeping until we are ready to deal with the content.

Several years ago I realized I had many characteristics of an adult with attention deficit disorder. This self-diagnosis may have been my own way of preservation, and it probably helped keep my stomach free of ulcers. I remember the day I finally realized I was an adult with ADD. I walked out of the bedroom and into the living room. I looked at my wife and told her I was still mad at her, but I couldn't remember why. It was probably best that my data buckets had several holes in the bottom, allowing data to slip away.

I had the ability to overlook things because I could not remember what happened. However, there is a difference between not remembering and having wisdom to overlook things. *Webster's Dictionary* describes "wisdom" as "the quality of being wise; good judgment, learning; knowledge, wise teaching."

Often, I have heard the expression that life is 5 percent what happens to you and 95 percent how you react. We all have the ability to decide how we will react to every situation. Our reaction determines the level and subsequent damage of the enemy attack.

Pick Your Battles

If your life is like mine, you will have plenty of opportunities for head-to-head combat. Battles are not always bad. Many great things we enjoy in our life are a result of someone's battle.

Constantly fighting battles, however, will lessen your effectiveness and weaken your defenses. That is why it is important to pick your battles. Only you can determine what battles you are willing to take on and what situations are worth overlooking.

The criteria I use is based on a three simple areas:

1. Eternal
2. External
3. Internal

What will be the lasting, long-term impact on these areas? Will fighting a battle cause long-term damage? Another key word in the criteria is "long-term." We need to learn what areas are worth the battle and what areas are just annoyances and will soon pass unnoticed. When we consider the worthiness of a battle affecting an "eternal" outcome, I will always fight until the end. Our time on this earth is so short compared to our time in eternity. Based on my beliefs, if the situation has an obvious eternal effect, put on the gloves and go to town.

Battles over "external" issues can easily be defined. Whether or not a situation can cause physical harm, property damage or some type of financial pain is fairly easily defined.

The most difficult situation to define is a battle that causes "internal" damage. It can be damage to our own interpersonal self but also damage to somebody else's self-perception.

As mentioned earlier, I let someone else dictate to me how I perceived myself. As parents, we have a huge responsibility to make sure that our words and actions do not cause damage to the self-worth of our children. We not only need to protect our "internal" self-concepts, but we need to nurture the self-worth of those people we care about.

Don't Overlook Everything!

I have been a part of many organizations whose traditional approach has been to overlook everything. Their basic philosophy was to ignore the problem and hope it would go away. Often this happens in the area of public opinion or concern.

One area many employers seem to overlook is employee behavior and work habits. I can tell you from experience that overlooking behavior can only lead to future problems. I have seen many organizations that have been forced to take costly actions because they failed to consider the consequences of their nonactions.

The State of Oklahoma statutes only allows school districts to hire employees on one-year contracts. First-year employees can be dismissed without a due process hearing at the end of the contract year. In other words, we can terminate their employment prior to their one-year anniversary and not be required to have a due process hearing for an employee wanting to appeal the decision.

We had an employee who had violated many policies that could result in immediate termination. We were sensitive to the financial plight of the employee, so we decided to wait and just nonrenew the employee at the end of the school year. Shortly after the completion of the school year, we were notified of the former employee's application for unemployment. I knew this was a slam-dunk because of all of the rules violations during the course of the school year.

I lost the hearing! In twenty-two years of people management, this was the first time I ever lost an unemployment hearing. The hearing judge stated that if the violations were severe enough for termination, the employee needed to be terminated at the time of the infraction, not at the end of the year.

Sometimes being nice just doesn't pay. You can't overlook everything.

CHAPTER 5

Sow Song

Anti-Idiotology #4:
Don't Attempt to Teach a Pig to Sing. It Can't Be Done and It Irritates the Pig! And Yet, Sometimes the Pig Needs to Learn to Sing!

This anti-idiotology is different from the first four because it is an offensive theory, not a preventive tactic.

When I was in college and many of the classrooms had desks with a small writing area on the right-hand side, I had to find two empty desks side by side so I could take notes. We live in a right-handed world. Being left-handed has its challenges!

I'm not making excuses for my abilities as a "handyman," but until I was thirty-three, the only tools I owned were a hammer, a multi-head screwdriver and a rusty saw. I had become very frustrated because of my lack of skill with tools.

If I had a slogan for my skills it would be, "I've cut the piece of wood three times and it is still too short." Some people just do not have the ability to accomplish a specific task.

Attempting to teach me carpenter skills was like teaching a pig to sing. I didn't want to know how to work on the house. I knew it would always cost us a lot more to call a professional to fix my messes, and I usually ended up with some type of injury before the project was over. When I worked on the house, I was irritated the entire time.

My skills, or the lack thereof, were well known to my staff. Every Monday I would recreate the escapades from my repairman follies. One year, as a thoughtful Christmas present, they gave me a toolbox with several tools. That, combined with a plumber telling my wife we were wasting our money paying him for doing repairs I could do, and I knew it was time for this southpaw to learn a few things about home repair.

Since that time, I have almost completely remodeled part of our house, including tile work and countertops. I have replaced bathroom vents, installed sinks, toilets and ceiling fans. I still get injured, but I am quite the handyman.

Sometimes we attempt to put people in positions that are not suitable to their skills and abilities, and they react to our actions with personal attacks and general dislike. It's common to have people mad at you because they are being challenged to perform a task they do not believe they are capable of accomplishing. They also get upset when their environment is changed or adjusted in a way in which they do not feel comfortable.

Secret Change Agent Man

One thing I have learned over the years is that change is inevitable, but in some cases, it must be slow, calculated and deliberate.

As the director of child nutrition for the Ponca City, Oklahoma, schools, I have always been a change agent. It was important for me to direct the organization to the edge of the envelope. I wanted to be the trendsetter. I wanted our program to be different in every aspect. Something strange got inside my brain that caused a serious malfunction. The idea came to me in a dream. (It must have been one of those late-night burritos right before bedtime.)

I dreamt the entire cafeteria staff was wearing tie-dyed shirts as uniforms. I woke up the next day and thought this idea would really work. See, this was far from the type of uniform we were wearing, and I just wanted some shock value for the students and staff. I thought it would be fun and...the employees, they would just love them...and they were colorful and the kids they would think that!

Well, I was wrong. Big time. I mean, not just underestimating the lack of acceptance, but totally overlooking the obvious appeal of the tie-dyed look.

The average age of our staff was probably mid-fifties. The look was all wrong for them. What was wrong with me? What made me think that they would want to wear these shirts and feel good in them?

Needless to say, I see these shirts at garage sales all over town.

Not to compare the staff to pigs, but metaphorically, these pigs did not want to sing, and I irritated them. Sometimes, we need to look at how we affect other people with changes or expectations. We need to determine if what we are asking of people is achievable. Otherwise, we may just irritate the pig by forcing them to see the world through our eyes.

Sometimes the *pig needs to learn to sing.* Sometimes we have to do things that take us out of our comfort zone, or attempt to accomplish things that have failed in the past.

I have learned that when I force change on people, they oppose the change, no matter how good it may be for them.

We have to decide whether or not their opposition is due to their total inability to accomplish the objective, or if it is just change they oppose.

Sometimes the pig cannot learn to sing and sometimes the pig needs to just be irritated until it learns to sing.

CHAPTER 6

Ouch, That Hurts

Anti-Idiotology #5:
Sticks and Stones May Break Your Bones, But Let's Stop Pretending Words Will Never Hurt You!

I was speaking at a church one Sunday, presenting a compelling message about the plight of many of the people in Eastern Europe. Prior to the service, I became aware of a young man who was autistic. He would repeat the word "Batman" periodically. Each time it would get a little louder, then work its way back to a whisper.

Several times during my message, I heard the word "Batman" repeated over and over. One time it was very loud and I paused for a moment to not laugh. Shortly after that, I heard him say, "I'll be quiet, I'll be quiet." A few moments later I heard the word "Batman" again. All of a sudden everyone could hear the sound of skin being smacked, followed by a loud "Ouch, that hurts!"

As with life, the pain followed the words. The young man fell prey to the hand because of his words.

Idiots have a way of inflicting damage by firing word

missiles. We try to play the John Wayne, Green Beret, commando, tough-guy role. "Words don't hurt me, they just roll right off of me."

Horse hockey! Double horse hockey!!! Words *do* hurt, and they leave a lasting impact.

Throughout history, the greatest weapon ever used was the tongue. Militaries have been mobilized, kingdoms have been launched, duels have been fought and relationships have been built and destroyed. This incredible organ has the ability to change the world.

Could I be giving this little muscle more credit than it deserves? Absolutely not!

Do we allow the tongue to totally dictate how we react, feel about ourselves and view the world? We sure do!

Of all of the Anti-Idiotologies, this is the toughest for me. I find it very difficult to overcome the effects of words. It has been a constant struggle to receive correction properly or to not let pointed criticism get under my skin. We all want to believe we have the answers and others should see things the way we do. Wanting to be right is just a natural part of everyday life.

The problem is we allow our pride to block out real truths that may be helpful to our personal development. We also let others dictate how we feel about ourselves.

Since we cannot control what other people say, the only words we should really care about are the ones coming out of our mouths. In reality, the phrase "sticks and stones may break my bones, but words will never hurt me," should be changed to "stick and stones may break my bones, but my own words could kill me."

How many times have we wanted "take backs" when

word missals have left our mouths unescorted by any type of logic? Good people forgive, but most never forget. Think of the times when it has taken years to get back in the good graces of someone after you have fired off a loaded bazooka of words in their direction.

We will never be able to control the words of others, but we can control our own words and weigh the potential damage of things that probably do not need to be stated.

If you ever have started a sentence with "I don't mean to hurt your feelings. but..." then you most likely *do* mean to hurt their feelings. Another way to say this would be, "You might not like what you're are getting ready to hear, but I think that you need to know that..." You may not intend to be mean or unkind, but you know before you deliver the comment what you are going to say will hurt them.

Don't think I am buying into the politically correct movement of tiptoeing around every issue. In our hypersensitive society, we have to calculate everything we say. I believe that there are many issues that need to be discussed openly and honestly in public. Public dialogue is critical to a free society, and stimulates ideas and understanding on all issues. I've met many people who want you to listen to their point of view on life, but they will not allow you to express your view.

The basic point of this "anti-idiotology" is to understand that words do hurt. Quit pretending they do not.

We need to calculate our comments and deal with the incoming comments from others.

Remember, broken bones heal in time. Words live on throughout time.

you CAN COUNT on us!
HANG ON, WE WILL GET YOU DOWN AFTER LUNCH!
R.SMITH

CHAPTER 7

And You Are...?

Anti-Idiotology #6:
Don't Rely on Those Who
Do Not Care About You!

I coached Little League baseball for many years. It was an experience I would not trade for anything. I could never replace the value lessons I learned through coaching. I am not the type of coach who has to win, although it's always nice to win a few games. One year a tie would have been something to hang my coaching hat on.

I had coached one group of boys for a couple of years. They had major potential—in academics, not sports. Somehow our team had no older players, limited experience in the league and average skill. We paid our dues that year.

We gave it our best shot but fell short in every game. Sometimes we fell just a hair short and some games we just won't talk about the outcome.

I had a good group of assistant coaches. They were energetic and very helpful. (At least we could spread the blame among all of the coaches.)

After the season was over, I gathered all of the coaches and asked if they were going to coach again the next year. We all agreed that we would have an older, more mature and experienced team. It was worth another shot and we should fare much better than we did this year.

During the off-season I would see the other coaches and joke about coaching again. We would laugh about the record and encourage each other about the upcoming anticipated season.

Finally, the time rolled around again to sign up to coach. I made my way to the sporting goods store, signed up my son to play and volunteered to coach the same team as I did for the last year couple of years.

Several weeks later when the coaches were notified of their players, I was surprised to find out I had only four guys from the previous team—my son, an assistant coach's son and two other players who really struggled during the previous year. I asked the commissioner of the league if there was a mistake and to check on specific names and the other assistant coaches.

Much to my disappointment, I found out that two of the assistant coaches from the previous year and the starting pitcher's dad had decided they would take the good players from the team and see if they could do better.

I asked the commissioner about the other names on the team. He stated they were players from various elementary schools who were not on their "neighborhood team." I asked the commissioner if these were players the other teams did not request to be on their roster, and he reluctantly agreed it could be possible this might have happened.

He also asked me to co-coach with another coach who had trouble with players' parents in the past. For some crazy reason, I agreed to this incredible mission of coaching the so-called uncoachable. I attached the enduring pet nickname of the "Bad News Rangers" to the team.

On the way to the first practice, my son asked me why the other kids from last year were not on our team and why we were driving across town to practice. I really couldn't give him an honest answer. I tried to be like a politician and say a lot, but not say anything. "The other kids needed a coach, and...well, I thought you would like the change in scenery." He didn't buy that line.

Then he asked, "Is it because we lost all of those games last year and the four who are on our team from last year are not very good?"

"Why do you say that?" I inquired.

Jordan looked me in the eye and said, "That is what the kids at school told me."

I knew then I had to make it very clear to all of the team of their value. Before practice began, I looked the players in the eye and began to explain how our team was formed. I was honest with them.

I told them some people did not believe they had the skills to be good enough to play on their team. "Some people believe this team will never win a game.

"But the other coaches and myself, believe that each one of you has the potential to be excellent play-ers—better than anyone in the league." It's a good thing

I was not Pinocchio, because my nose would have grown so fast it could have been used for a bat.

The other coach chimed in and said, "We care about you. We want you to be successful, and we will see to it that you are winners."

What a novel concept! Take a group of players, who have learned a very pointed lesson in life, and let them know they will be successful, because we care enough about them to do everything we can to help them succeed.

Needless to say, that season was extremely enjoyable. Each game showed a glimpse of improvement. Then, we started winning. Somehow, someway we found a way to win.

The team began to believe in themselves and it became interesting to see how they would respond. They began to walk with a swagger. They would encourage each other. They had fun. Our team finished in the top half of a very difficult league.

A great lesson to learn from this story is that when people care about you, they make sure you succeed. So many times we rely on those who do not care about the success of the organization. They just care about themselves and their agenda. Oftentimes we make the error of relying on people who do not care about us. They are not team players and they quietly do what they can to slowly erode other individuals' support for the success of the project.

We constantly put valuable pieces of our organizations in the hands of people who are not team players. They do not share the vision or goals of the leadership.

What really is ironic is the fact that we act surprised when they turn on the organization when things don't go their way.

Why do we believe it is our purpose to provide jobs, that our organizations are fronts to fulfill some type of "employment service" for the rebellious spirits to have something to do during the day? All organizations need to realize team players can make an organization successful, and non–team players can rip the organization apart at the seams.

In order to fight these secret operative idiot attacks, we must constantly monitor the pulse of the organization. We have to always keep the lines of communication open and confront and evaluate feedback from the staff. We cannot be afraid to ask why support is being doubted and weakened. Once we get an understanding, we need to make a clear statement of support and make adjustments when needed.

Frequently, people who work against the organization begin their "subversive" mission when they do not feel valued or feel they can do a better job of leading the organization. Much like the "Bad News Rangers," once they realize their value, they began to work as a team.

Whether it is a business, an organization or a ball team, we need to realize when people are valued, they respond. However, we need to understand that placing the success of your organization in the hands of those who don't care about you could result in a major mess.

The Bad News Rangers beat the team that spurned them, and the players the other team didn't want scored the winning runs. I guess happy endings are not just for fairy tales.

CHAPTER 8

What Would It Hurt to Ask?

Anti-Idiotology #7:
If YOU Are Not Prepared for the Answer "No," Don't Ask the Question!

Why do we do this to ourselves all of the time?

It's a passionate issue. We believe strongly in our opinion. Our hopes, dreams and self-worth hinge on this specific issue. In order to build up the courage to take on the topic we self-talk ourselves into taking the first step.

It's as if we are getting to take an early spring dive into a swimming pool; we stand on the side of the pool and stare at the cold water. Finally, without any specific prompting, we jump in fast and get it over with.

The self-talk begins. I will just ask, that's all. If the answer is "no," then I will move on. At least I asked!

49

What's the harm of asking? Hey, all I can do is ask!

As if being shot out of a cannon you burst into their office.

You have practiced this speech a hundred times. Guns loaded. (Figuratively speaking.)

Here it goes. You blurt out your position on this issue.

It's a masterful presentation. Not a dry eye in the place.

They ease up in their chair. Fold their hands in front of their chest. Look you right in the eye. And in a delicate, gentle and loving way, they utter the word, "No!"

You are shocked. Could you possibly be hearing this correctly?

"No! What do you mean no?" *Why you low-life crust on the belly of a scorpion. How dare you disagree with me? After all I have done for you. I have given you the best years of my life, and this is how you show me your appreciation.*

I am going to make sure everyone I come into contact with knows how low you are. I will tell everyone that you are so unfeeling, unprofessional and most of all, wrong.

I can't believe it that you do not see it my way. How do you live with yourself?

Now hold on just a minute.

Didn't you say, "All I could do is ask"? "What would it hurt"?

The problem is that many times we self-talk ourselves into taking a bold stand on issues that are dear to us, and we use motivation by reassuring ourselves that if we don't get our way, it won't be a big deal.

Then, we play the victim when we don't get our way. It's funny, we don't tolerate this behavior out of our children, but we patronize adults when they behave in the same way.

We give them an audience. We help tell their sad story to others. We reassure them that they are fine in thinking that they are a victim. We are enablers. We enable these people to turn our offices, homes and relationships upside-down because they did not get their way.

A Surprise Attack

Many public schools advance the annual pay of every employee through a step system. It has absolutely nothing to do with merit. It is totally based on tenure and category. I guess our focus is more on being fair than being productive.

My duties as chief financial officer involve maintaining the step schedule and making "wholesale" increases or the establishment of a new category. Advancing a single employee is not an option, unless he or she changed positions or classification.

One day an employee made an appointment to discuss her salary. I knew there was nothing I could do to place her in another category or increase her steps, but I agreed to listen to her concern. She began the conversation by saying, "I figured it didn't hurt to ask." I relaxed my demeanor and attempted to explain the district's position on only advancing steps based on tenure and not merit. She asked if I could create a separate category for her, and I explained her responsibilities were not much different from the others in the same category. A bit of small talk followed, then she stated again it didn't hurt to ask. The meeting ended and I moved on to something else.

Unbeknownst to me, my refusal to increase her wages fueled a fire that escalated into a very miserable couple of years. I spent a lot of time defending her verbal allegations of wrongdoing. She attempted to plant a seed of scorn in the minds of many of the people I supervised. She was determined to make me pay for not valuing her in the organization.

She succeeded in making my life miserable. I never knew when the next attack would occur. She doubled as my friend, yet threw darts at my back on every occasion. All of this because she was not prepared for the answer "no."

If we are not ready for the answer "no," we need to evaluate our position and determine the basis of our passion. Is it an emotional attachment, or is it a moral or legal question? Does our "pride" get in the way of our logic, or do we really think that our life will end if we don't get our way?

Ask anyone who knows me well and they will agree with the statement that I have an opinion. I often joke that there will be two statements on my tombstone: "He Had an Opinion" and "I Told You I Was Sick."

I believe in a passionate support of many causes. I won't back off on what I hold dear. However, I have to ask myself all of the time, What is the worst thing that will happen if I hear the answer "no"?

Where is it written that if someone else disagrees with us, they are wrong? What's wrong with being wrong sometimes? Does it mean we should live in shame for the rest of our lives? Does it mean we are always wrong? Or is it just stubborn pride?

There is a difference between disappointment and anger. We need to rehearse our position and the possible answer. Weigh our responses and evaluate our true motivation for our specific position.

E-Force

Recently, a well-meaning teacher who was questioning the nutritional integrity of our child nutrition program confronted me via e-mail. She copied the e-mail to many people who were not a part of the system, which I found very upsetting. Her tone and approach to the topic was abrupt. It could have been a marriage proposal and I would have been upset.

I was totally blown away with her questions. After sending a nice, yet firm response, I soon realized I had probably provoked her to anger. She didn't like being wrong and neither did I.

We both held our positions until I ended the sparring match with the statement, "I consider discussion of this issue finished." How dare she question what I have done? The nerve of her insisting on nutritional accountability for our child nutrition program. Granted, her approach was wrong, but my response was worse. I let her get under my skin. Pride got in the way of my sense of understanding. Rather than take a time of self-examination, I responded with an attitude of arrogance. It really, really felt good.

A few days later I struck up a conversation with one of the people she had included in our e-mail battle. She made a comment about the encounter, and I felt safe to divulge my true feelings about the content. Much to my surprise, this person began to articulate the same argument, but she made sense. Because of her approach and demeanor, I received the sincere concern and began a plan to make adjustments. I soon realized my position could be wrong and her concerns genuine.

Later, I apologized to the teacher for my response, explaining that my knee-jerk reaction may have been due in part to her approach.

We choose our responses to situations. We choose to be offended, hurt and upset. I chose my response and had a multi-day pity party. It was fun but became way too difficult to maintain.

I had to avoid her and not make eye contact when we met. It was too much work.

If we can't handle the answer, then we probably need not ask the question until we can deal with what we do not want to hear. This is not easy, but it can be done. Sometimes "no" is the right answer.

Go Get 'Em, Coach

Anti-Idiotology #8:
*Don't Assume the Idiots Know
You Are Referring to Them,
Because They Never Take
Responsibility for Anything!*

I received my degree in hotel and restaurant administration. This is a unique degree because it offers a wide variety of totally different career opportunities. Often, our class would feature a guest speaker from the industry. I remember a country club general manager speaking to our class. During the question-and-answer period, a student asked him about the major drawback of country club management. His reply was that in country club management, customers are under the true belief they own you. I did not like that option, so I tried to stay as far away from that type of management as I could.

I must have forgotten my dislike for that theory when I decided to go into public education. That is where everyone *really* thinks they own you.

Much to my surprise, I really do like this field, but it is made up of many "storied" individuals. Many of the administrators for small school districts are former coaches. So, it is not unusual to go to a meeting and hear everyone referred to as "coach." In fact, my superintendent calls me "coach." When we get into a tough situation, he always says, "Go get 'em, coach." I head out the door with a snort full of enthusiasm and vigor. I'm ready to take on the problem until I realize the idiots don't know I am talking about them. They usually assume I am addressing everyone but them.

I also follow the golden rule of management: I treat people how I want to be treated. This could be good or bad. Some people like the gentle mink glove of encouragement and others just want it to be direct and to the point.

I used to use a very basic theory of management called the "buckshot" approach. Now remember, I said "used to." This theory means you address problems to all staff members and let the guilty ones hear it without getting singled out. I guess I learned this by being raised in the church. You know, the pastor gets up there and preaches his heart out, and if it applies to you, take it and make a change. If it doesn't, then pray for those who need the help.

It took me several years to realize this theory does not work very well. It was obvious IT was not effective. The first sign was a lack of improvement on behalf of the guilty party. It was like we never had the discussion. The second was about as subtle when a group of managers approached me and asked why they always get the lecture, whether or not they were even involved in the situation. I really could not tell them why I used this method of management. Maybe it was fear or not wanting to embarrass anyone in front of their peers.

If you have grown up with multiple siblings, you know how this feels. Someone else messes up and you all get in trouble. Line up and you all get the belt.

It finally dawned on me the subtle buckshot approach did not work at all. It's like the military bombing an entire country, just to get one small group of people. I guess the buzzword is *collateral damage*. How do you get the target without causing problems for everyone else?

The remedy is simple. You have to make two major assumptions.

First, the idiots do not know you are talking about them.

They really don't. When you are addressing the problem, they sit there and nod their heads and say, "Go get 'em, coach." It's as if they are totally oblivious to the entire conversation. Then, when you confront them, they seem to be in a state of disbelief. This brings us to the second assumption: Idiots don't take responsibility for their own actions.

Have you ever been around someone who is never wrong? They just don't make any mistakes. Now, I have been accused of this before, but surely it's because of my confidence in my opinion. Yeah, that's it...I'm just confident I could not have made a mistake.

Honestly, we all make mistakes. It's a bummer when we do and it's hard to admit it. However, idiots cannot even admit they could be wrong. They always have an excuse. They justify their position.

I can tell you why I want to be right all the time. I'm insecure with myself. Plain and simple. I'm tired of being wrong. I need success. There I said it; now I can move on.

We see ourselves in a totally different light than others. The other day, I walked by my secretary and said something. She asked me if I was okay because I seemed a little grumpy. "Grumpy? What do you mean 'grumpy'? Me grumpy? The happiest, most positive and upbeat person in the world? How can I be grumpy?"

Several years ago, our staff received a special training for handling people who are unhappy with the school district. It was based on identifying the personality type of the individual who was upset and reacting to them in a positive way they would understand and respect. A part of the training was to identify your personality type so you can see how your type affects the other person's personality. Each type was assigned a color that was matched against another color. Your response would be based on the two colors. I know this is confusing, but it really works.

After the training, I was able to see how many of the employees ranked themselves. I was amazed with how people really perceived themselves. I could see they were under the assumption they were not the person being addressed. They truly see themselves in a totally different light.

My children were listening to their voices on a tape recorder and both were convinced it was someone else speaking. My daughter said, "Okay, Daddy, tell me whose voice that really was." She was so sure it was not her voice.

Recently, an employee had to be reprimanded for not coming in on time, taking long lunches and leaving early. When confronted about the concerns, she denied this was happening. To this day she believes she was at her desk. There are a lot of things you can deny, but your presence at your desk is measurable.

Constant self-evaluation is always necessary. We need to be aware of our words and actions.

After an innocent conversation with a teacher had escalated into a big mess, I asked an administrator where I made my mistake.

His answer was very simple. "You thought you were dealing with a rational person."

I laughed at his reply. However, it is true. We need to be aware of the total environment, personality and mental awareness of the people we are addressing. This will help in being effective when communicating with the idiotic behavior.

R. Smith

CHAPTER 10

I'm Ba-ack!

Anti-Idiotology #9:
If You Think Ignoring Them Will Make Them Go Away, Think Again!

In the classic movie *Poltergeist,* the little girl with blonde hair gazes into the television and calmly states, "They're back." Everyone thought they were gone, but the poltergeists did return for the final destruction of the house.

I am not a confrontational person. I will walk a mile out of my way to avoid a confrontation with someone. I just don't like it. It gives me a knotting, gnarling, sinking, sick kind of feeling in my gut. I never feel good after a disagreement. So, many times I pretend the problem just goes away. It just vanishes. Goodbye, trouble, goodbye. So long, headache. So long, misery. As long as I can't see it, the problem must be solved.

When my children were little, I would play hide-and-seek with them. It was so funny. They would hide their faces behind some object or wall. They thought that as long as they could not see me, I could not see them.

As adults, we act the same way. Maybe if we ignore it, the problem will go away. If we just hide our heads in a pillow, no one will bother us.

We have all been there. Those days when we get hit from all sides.

Product failures, physical and employee problems bomb us all at once. We don't know which way to run, so we fight off the hardest hits and let the others sit there and simmer until we are ready to deal with them. But secretly, we hope the problem either solves itself or just goes away. Unfortunately, this rarely happens.

Once a problem, always a problem. The chance of the situation just fixing itself is very unlikely. Just like autos, appliances and computers, problems rarely fix themselves.

Nose Candy

In a brief moment of insanity, my wife and I purchased a deli and candy store, which was located in our downtown business district. The week following the purchase of the existing business, the major local employer laid off 900 of their employees. We were located close to their offices and we had to change plans, so this was devastating to the business.

Rather than a new beginning with the business, I decided to retain a few of the employees and reopen the remodeled business as fast as I could. One of the employees was in desperate need of a job, so I used her in many capacities.

When the manager was out, this employee would operate the store and also act as cashier. Because I maintained my job with the school district, I was unable to spend much time during the day with the business. I had to really trust everyone to take care of the business properly.

Unknown to me, the cash drawer would come up short almost every day. When I read the end of month statement, I thought it was "over rings" or just poor change making.

One day, a friend of the family contacted me and said she had been in for lunch and noticed an employee had walked over to the register to make change. Before she closed the drawer, she looked around the room, then took out a twenty-dollar bill and placed it in her pocket.

I was shocked. Surely, this employee would not be stealing from us! After all, she needed a job, and she had become our friend.

After much painful deliberation, I decided I would just ask her if she was stealing from the business. I expected her to voice a very bold denial and feeling of outrage. Much to my surprise, she broke down and started crying. She told me she was addicted to cocaine and desperate for help. She also stated if she lost her job for stealing, it would violate her parole and she would have to go back to jail and would probably lose custody of her kids.

Not only was I shocked by her admission of theft, I was also surprised she had a previous record. But I was touched by her honesty. Her sincerity was so genuine. I wanted to help her straighten up her life. She became my project.

I assisted her in getting counseling for her addiction. I attempted to get her "plugged in" to a local church. She was well on the road to recovery.

One afternoon, I received a call from a check-cashing establishment in a neighboring community. They were whispering, so it was difficult for me to understand what they were saying. I finally began to understand they were asking if it was possible my wife was in their community cashing a check.

I responded that she was working next door to the deli at another business. They asked me to describe my wife and I told them she had blonde hair and blue eyes. They said I probably had a problem then, because there was a female with dark hair and dark eyes at their business stating that she was my wife and wanted to cash a rather large check.

I was outraged. How could this happen? They gave me a more detailed description and I knew exactly who it was. The check-cashing company gave me the number of the check, and I immediately went to the business and tried to figure out how this employee would have gotten her hands on the check.

I opened the checkbook and soon realized the check number was much higher than the checks in the front. She had removed a check from the back of the book, so we would not notice it for a long time. She had planned to be long gone by the time we found out her check-stealing plan.

I honestly thought her theft problem would just go away. I had put her on notice, and I thought she was on the road to recovery. Wrong!

Second chances are what makes the world go around, but we can't fool ourselves into believing that things fix themselves. Sometimes we have to make very difficult decisions. We have to get out of our comfort zones and look the problems in the eye.

All too often in the public sector, we spend more time managing the appearance of things, rather than the real problems. We seek damage control instead of remedy. And we usually end up in the same situation as we were earlier, only their missiles have caused much greater damage than if we would have looked them in the eye when the problem first began. We seek the easy, peaceful and politically correct solutions, rather than doing the right thing for the betterment of the organization.

Handling problems head-on may be painful, but better now than later, when the damage is much more severe and costly.

Believe me, I know about this one. If you think that ignoring them will make them go away, think again.

CHAPTER 11

Today's Special Is Rump Roast!

Anti-Idiotology #10:
If There Is a Chance It Could Bite You In the Butt, It Will!

I saved the best one for last. I probably quote this "bite your butt" statement several times a week. But it is so true. In life, things have a tendency to just chomp right down on the hindquarters.

A wise person once said, "A sharp tongue will cut your own throat."

When I was growing up, I remember our pastor saying, "Now, I don't want ya'll going home and have roasted preacher for lunch." I always thought that was funny, but I really didn't know what he meant. Now I do.

Our words and actions have a tendency to come back to us.

First of all, this "idiotology" was created because many things in my life have come back to haunt me. Things I could not have imagined would have amounted to anything have snowballed themselves into big messes. Some of those comments or actions were very innocent in nature and others could have been easily avoided.

If you are tired of things coming back to take a chomp out of your end zone, here is a basic rule of thumb to aid in minimizing casualties from innocent remarks. It is called the THINK checkoff system. It is very easy.

When you take an action or make a statement, make sure it meets these criteria. Is it...*T*ruthful? *H*elpful? *I*nspirational? *N*ecessary? *K*ind?

There was an incident many years ago that brings back a lot of laughter and a few regrets. I am not sure how I could have avoided this incident, other than just not doing it at all, but it was very funny.

We always tried to do something unique to celebrate birthdays. In fact, it became a contest to see who could outdo the other. There had to be some shock value and some risk. One of our managers was having a birthday, and she always joked about the ladies in the kitchen hiring a stripper to come in and dance for her birthday, but we knew that it probably would not be a good idea because we worked in a school.

During the morning break, they decided to blindfold her, place her in an office chair in the middle of the cafeteria and pretend a real stripper had been hired to strip for her birthday. While the music was being played on the tape player, someone from the group would place specific items of clothing on her head and lap, indicating the stripper was really disrobing. Then, when the music was over, the blindfold would be removed and she would see it was a joke.

Well, for some stupid reason, I volunteered to be the one to place the garments on her while the music was playing. I really wanted to get her good, so I decided to dress up in a ridiculous costume, and when the blind fold was removed, she would realize it had been me the entire time.

I put on a colorful pair of boxer shorts, boots, long sleeve underwear shirt and a cowboy hat. I really looked hideous.

The plan went along without a hitch. The music was loud, the lunch ladies were screaming and whistling and the birthday girl was having a ball. In fact, the ladies were having so much fun it attracted a special education class into the dining area. Everyone was clapping and having a ball.

As planned, the song ended and the blindfold was removed. Everyone cheered at the birthday girl being tricked into thinking that a gorgeous stripper was her birthday entertainment, but in reality it really looked like someone who had just crawled off of the turnip truck.

Much to everyone's surprise, including the birthday girl's and myself, for some reason, when her blindfold was removed, she decided to pull down my boxers.

I guess you could say it was the last thing I expected. Everyone in the room gasped because the pulling down of the boss's boxers was not that common.

We all laughed and I recovered and covered as fast as I could.

However, the special education teacher was not amused by the incident. In fact, she was really upset. (I don't know why—her students laughed as much as everyone else.) She wrote a letter to the superintendent at the time and all of the board members. She also sent a letter to a man who was campaigning to be a new member of the school board. Needless to say, I was called into the superintendent's office and received a reprimand for my lapse of judgment.

The guy running for the school board did not see it as funny as the rest of us did. In fact, I think he used the incident in his campaign.

I had to make a public apology for my behavior, and it took me several years before our newly elected board member could trust me again.

That's right. Big ole' chunk out of the glutes (of the maximus persuasion). Things just happen. Some can be avoided and others can't.

All we can do is make sure we use the THINK checkoff and we realize on any occasion, things can come back to you.

CHAPTER 12

A War to End All Wars

The ten anti-idiotologies have even evolved during the writing of this book. It just goes to show that this will be a constant, never-ending battle.

But isn't life?

As stated earlier, life is 5 percent of what happens to us, and 95 percent how we respond.

I hope this book has demonstrated how we set ourselves up for emotional damage when we tolerate certain types of behavior from not only others, but ourselves.

Could it be that many of you have read this book to assist you in dealing with the idiots and soon found out you have more control over situations than you thought? I have spent a lifetime digging myself out of problems I probably could have avoided, if I would have handled the situation a little differently.

However, I also realize sometimes things just happen.

I always lean on the scripture that God does not give us any more than we can handle. I really do believe our experiences only make us stronger and better.

Whether it is dealing with people we don't re-spect, having others' moods dictate our self-worth, knowing when to quit or continue, or maybe the way we pretend people's words don't hurt us, we need to understand how our decisions affect ourselves and others.

After we learn it is tough to rely on people who don't care about you, and how to know if we are ready for the answer "no," we might start to see progress in our relationships. We have to understand that the idiots don't know we are referring to them, and ig-noring them only gives them more time to make a better plan.

Finally, the possibility will always exist for our words, actions and best intentions turning on us and just biting the fire out of our behinds.

Life is a great journey. It's fun, exciting, sad and tiring. Make the road trip an enjoyable experience.

Don't let the idiots win!

BIBLIOGRAPHY

Chameleon. *Microsoft® Encarta® Online Encyclopedia 2001,* http://encarta.msn.com (December 3, 2001).

Webster's New World Dictionary, Modern Desk Edition. New York: Simon and Schuster,1979.

ABOUT THE AUTHOR

It is no coincidence Jeff Denton was born in Roswell, New Mexico, right around the time the UFO sightings occurred. Even his mother wonders if there was any link to his birth and the alleged alien visits. Shortly after his birth in Roswell, his family moved to Ponca City, Oklahoma, a postcard of Americana at its best.

The Denton family experience mirrored Ward and June Cleaver, with Jeff as "the Beaver." The middle son of a dad who was an oil company geophysicist and a mom who was an avid professional volunteer, Jeff learned the importance of service to others. His youngest brother, born with Down's syndrome, added love, life and laughter to the home.

Politically active at eight years old, Jeff championed liberal and conservative causes with passion and enthusiasm. Often, as an adolescent and teen-ager, he authored editorials in the local newspaper. He definitely had an opinion.

After graduation from Oklahoma State University with a degree in Human Environmental Science, Jeff embarked on a career in the hospitality industry. In 1990, he returned to his hometown to work with Ponca City Public Schools. He currently serves as the chief financial officer for the school district.

As a champion for children and youths, Jeff serves on seven local, state and national boards, all in service to children and youth. He has led eleven teams to Eastern Europe to work in the schools and distribute Bibles to the students. Jeff also has served as a children's pastor and still wakes up in the middle of the night, yelling, "Is big church over yet?"

Married to Camille in 1986, Jeff's highlight and number-one love is being father to two beautiful, red-headed, blue-eyed children, Jordan and Madison. He is an avid college sports fan, Little League coach and keeper of the remote control. Like a goose, he wakes up in a new world every day.

Give the Gift of
Don't Let the Idiots Win!
to Your Friends and Colleagues

CHECK YOUR LEADING BOOKSTORE OR ORDER HERE

❑ YES, I want _____ copies of *Don't Let the Idiots Win!* at $9.95 each, plus $4.95 shipping per book (Oklahoma residents please add 45¢ sales tax per book). Canadian orders must be accompanied by a postal money order in U.S. funds. Allow 15 days for delivery.

❑ **YES**, I am interested in having Jeff Denton speak or give a seminar to my company, association, school, or organization. Please send information.

My check or money order for $_____ is enclosed.
Please charge my: ❑ Visa   ❑ MasterCard
                   ❑ Discover   ❑ American Express

Name _____

Organization _____

Address _____

City/State/Zip _____

Phone_____ E-mail _____

Card # _____

Exp. Date_____ Signature_____

Please make your check payable and return to:
Finishing Strong Productions
P.O. Box 773 • Ponca City, OK 74602
Call your credit card order to: 580-765-3345
Fax: 580-767-8007